THE COACH

The Heart Behind The Champion

by Patrick Caton

Cover Illustration by Design Dynamics
Typography by MarketForce, Burr Ridge, IL

Published by Great Quotations Publishing Co.,
Downers Grove, IL

Library of Congress Catalog Number: 98-77655

ISBN: 1-56245-339-4

Printed in Hong Kong 2001

DEDICATION

THIS BOOK IS DEDICATED TO ALL THE
COACHES IN MY LIFE WHO HELPED MAKE
ME MORE LIKE BRIAN CAREY.

INTRODUCTION

There are intangibles which seem to be common in all great coaches. Character, charisma and inner drive are just a few of the unique skills used by these men & women to transcend the X's & O's on a blackboard. They are able to harness the talents of individual athletes and merge them into one unified champion. As you read the quotes in this book, you will see the qualities and color which compel players and non-players alike to call them, "Coach".

Author's note: Because of the changing nature of coaching, which you will read about, I have tried to use the team which the coach was with at the time of the quote if the quote was topical. In all other cases, I used the team which he/she is best known for coaching.

Leadership

*Above all things, a coach must be a leader.
Athletes are unable to be more than the sum
of their parts without effective leadership.
The following quotations illustrate this quality
which allows the team to function as one unit.*

WHEN YOU MAKE A MISTAKE, THERE ARE ONLY THREE THINGS YOU SHOULD EVER DO ABOUT IT:

1. *ADMIT IT;*
2. *LEARN FROM IT AND*
3. *DON'T REPEAT IT.*

Paul "Bear" Bryant
University of Alabama Football

MOST COACHES STUDY THE FILMS WHEN THEY LOSE. I STUDY THEM WHEN WE WIN, TO SEE IF I CAN FIGURE OUT WHAT I DID RIGHT.

Paul "Bear" Bryant
University of Alabama Football

HE ALWAYS SAID THAT IF YOU FEEL LIKE YOU'RE GOING TO HIT INTO A DOUBLE PLAY, STRIKE OUT.

Don Baylor
Colorado Rockies
Recalling wisdom he received from Earl Weaver.

7

IF YOU DON'T BELIEVE IN YOURSELF, EVERYONE KNOWS IT. HOW CAN YOU LEAD THE CAVALRY IF YOU THINK YOU LOOK FUNNY SITTING ON A HORSE?

Hal McRae
Kansas City Royals

> *THE COUNTRY IS FULL OF GOOD COACHES. WHAT IT TAKES TO WIN IS A BUNCH OF INTERESTED PLAYERS.*

Don Coryell
San Diego Chargers

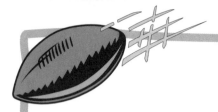

COACHES WHO CAN OUTLINE PLAYS ON A BLACKBOARD ARE A DIME A DOZEN. THE ONES WHO WIN GET INSIDE THEIR PLAYERS AND MOTIVATE.

Vince Lombardi
Green Bay Packers

LISTEN, I WAS THE FIRST BLACK MANAGER IN BASEBALL AND THERE WAS INCREDIBLE PRESSURE. I DON'T BLAME ANYONE ELSE. I WAS TOO TOUGH... I LACKED PATIENCE. BUT WE HAD A ROUGH SITUATION, TOO. IT WAS MY FIRST JOB AS A MANAGER AND I WANTED TO WIN—BADLY. I PROBABLY GOT ON GUYS A LITTLE TOO HARD, WITH THE WRONG TONE OF VOICE.

Frank Robinson
Baltimore Orioles

I COULDN'TA DONE IT WITHOUT MY PLAYERS.

Casey Stengel
New York Yankees

I LIKE MY PLAYERS TO BE MARRIED AND IN DEBT. THAT'S THE WAY YOU MOTIVATE THEM.

Ernie Banks
Chicago Cubs

13

WHAT YOU DO IN LIFE BY YOURSELF DOESN'T MEAN AS MUCH AS WHAT YOU ACCOMPLISH WITH A GROUP OF PEOPLE.

Mike Ditka
Chicago Bears

14

THE WAY I SEE IT, IS THAT'S PART OF FOOTBALL. THERE ARE GOING TO BE ARGUMENTS AND DIFFERENCES OF OPINION. A FOOTBALL TEAM IS LIKE YOUR FAMILY, AND IT'S SILLY TO THINK THERE WOULDN'T BE DISAGREEMENTS. NOW, THE IMPORTANT THING IS HOW YOU HANDLE IT. I DON'T LOSE MY TEMPER MUCH IN A TIME LIKE THAT. THOSE THINGS END UP BEING DISCUSSED IN ONE-ON-ONE MEETINGS. I'VE HAD HUNDREDS OF THOSE. THERE'S ALWAYS SOMETHING GOING ON INSIDE A TEAM. SOMEONE ALWAYS HAS SOMETHING ON THEIR MIND, AND I LIKE TO GET TO IT RIGHT AWAY. I DON'T LIKE TO GIVE THINGS TIME TO GET WORSE.

Joe Gibbs
Washington Redskins

15

I'M NOT BUDDY-BUDDY WITH THE PLAYERS. IF THEY NEED A BUDDY, LET THEM BUY A DOG.

Whitey Herzog
St. Louis Cardinals (Baseball)

*THE COACH IS THE TEAM,
AND THE TEAM IS THE COACH.
YOU REFLECT EACH OTHER.*

Sparky Anderson
Detroit Tigers

I BELIEVE IN RULES. SURE I DO. IF THERE WEREN'T ANY RULES, HOW COULD YOU BREAK THEM?

Leo Durocher
Chicago Cubs

18

A HEAD COACH IS GUIDED BY THIS MAIN OBJECTIVE: DIG, CLAW, WHEEDLE, COAX THAT FANATICAL EFFORT OUT OF THE PLAYERS. YOU WANT THEM TO PLAY EVERY SATURDAY AS IF THEY WERE PLANTING THE FLAG ON IWO JIMA.

Darrell Royal
University of Texas Football

19

*A TEAM HAS GOT TO HAVE QUICKNESS; IT'S GOT TO
HAVE A STRENGTH; IT'S GOT TO BE ABLE TO SHOOT
THE BALL. NOW, THE BETTER THEY ARE AT ANY
ONE OF THESE, OR ALL OF THEM, THE BETTER THE
TEAM IT CAN BE. THEN, THE NEXT MOST
IMPORTANT INGREDIENT IS SOME KIND OF DEPTH.
ONCE A TEAM BRINGS ANY OR ALL OF THOSE FOUR
INGREDIENTS TO THE FLOOR, THEN IT HAS TO BE
PUT TOGETHER. AND THAT'S WHERE COACHING
COMES INTO PLAY. THERE ARE A LOT OF TEAMS
THAT HAVE THE BASKETBALL INGREDIENTS, BUT JUST
NEVER GET PUT TOGETHER PROPERLY.*

Bobby Knight
University of Indiana Basketball

20

MY COACHING PHILOSOPHY IS THAT IT'S MY RESPONSIBILITY TO GET THE MOST OUT OF THE TALENT I HAVE TO WORK WITH. WHAT YOU HAVE TO DO IS DETERMINE WHAT THEIR TALENT IS, AND THEN GIVE THEM ALL OF THE WEAPONS THAT YOU CAN SO YOU CAN GET THE MOST OUT OF THEM.

Don Shula
Miami Dolphins

21

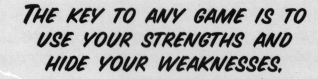

THE KEY TO ANY GAME IS TO USE YOUR STRENGTHS AND HIDE YOUR WEAKNESSES.

Paul Westphal
Phoenix Suns

22

> *WHEN I WAS COACHING, THE ONE THOUGHT THAT I WOULD TRY TO GET ACROSS TO MY PLAYERS WAS THAT EVERYTHING I DO EACH DAY, EVERYTHING I SAY, I MUST FIRST THINK WHAT EFFECT IT WILL HAVE ON EVERYONE CONCERNED.*

Frank Layden
Utah Jazz

I HAVE A BASIC PHILOSOPHY THAT I'VE TRIED TO FOLLOW DURING MY COACHING CAREER. WHETHER YOU'RE WINNING OR LOSING, IT IS IMPORTANT TO ALWAYS BE YOURSELF. YOU CAN'T CHANGE BECAUSE OF THE CIRCUMSTANCES AROUND YOU.

Cotton Fitzsimmons
Phoenix Suns

24

*I ALWAYS KNOW WHAT'S
HAPPENING ON THE COURT.
I SEE A SITUATION OCCUR,
AND I RESPOND.*

Larry Bird
Indianapolis Pacers

WHEN IT COMES TO THE FOOTBALL FIELD, MIND WILL ALWAYS WIN OVER MUSCLE AND BRUTE FORCE.

Walter Camp
Yale Football

THE SECRET OF WINNING FOOTBALL GAMES IS WORKING MORE AS A TEAM, LESS AS INDIVIDUALS. I PLAY NOT MY 11 BEST, BUT MY BEST 11.

Knute Rockne
Notre Dame Football

27

PRACTICE WITHOUT IMPROVEMENT IS MEANINGLESS.

Chuck Knox
Los Angeles Rams

BESIDES PRIDE, LOYALTY, DISCIPLINE, HEART AND MIND, CONFIDENCE IS THE KEY TO ALL THE LOCKS.

Joe Paterno
Pennsylvania State University Football

SUCCESS IS NEVER FINAL. FAILURE IS NEVER FATAL.

Joe Paterno
Pennsylvania State University Football

29

IT'S WHAT YOU LEARN AFTER YOU KNOW IT ALL THAT COUNTS.

John Wooden
UCLA Basketball

THINGS TURN OUT BEST FOR PEOPLE WHO MAKE THE BEST OF THE WAY THINGS TURN OUT.

John Wooden
UCLA Basketball

I THINK THE COACHES TEACHING YOUNGSTERS IN HIGH SCHOOL AND COLLEGE TODAY SHOULD BE REQUIRED TO PRACTICE A CERTAIN DECORUM. THEY'RE IN A LEADERSHIP ROLE, AND I THINK OUR YOUNGSTERS NEED MODELS MORE THAN THEY NEED CRITICISM. THERE HAVE BEEN SOME VERY SUCCESSFUL COACHES THAT HAVE BEEN VERY PROFANE. I DON'T BLAME THEM. I BLAME THE PEOPLE THAT HIRED THEM. IF YOU USED PROFANITY IN MY PRACTICE, YOU WERE OFF THE FLOOR FOR A DAY.

John Wooden
Talking about profanity in today's college basketball.

31

TELL A BALLPLAYER SOMETHING A THOUSAND TIMES, THEN TELL HIM AGAIN, BECAUSE THAT MIGHT BE THE TIME HE UNDERSTANDS SOMETHING.

Paul Richards
Baltimore Orioles

*I HAD NO TROUBLE COMMUNICATING.
THE PLAYERS JUST DIDN'T
LIKE WHAT I HAD TO SAY.*

Frank Robinson
Cleveland Indians

33

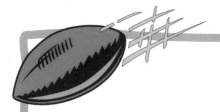

THERE ARE COACHES WHO SPEND 18 HOURS A DAY COACHING THE PERFECT GAME, AND THEY LOSE BECAUSE THE BALL IS OVAL AND THEY CAN'T CONTROL THE BOUNCE.

Bud Grant
Minnesota Vikings

I WANT MY TEAMS TO HAVE
MY PERSONALITY:
SURLY, OBNOXIOUS AND ARROGANT.

Al McGuire
Marquette Basketball

THE MAIN THING IS GETTING PEOPLE TO PLAY. WHEN YOU THINK IT'S YOUR SYSTEM THAT'S WINNING, YOU'RE IN FOR A DAMN BIG SURPRISE. IT'S THOSE PLAYERS' EFFORT.

Bum Phillips
Houston Oilers

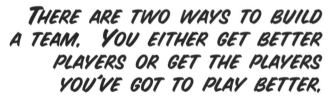

THERE ARE TWO WAYS TO BUILD A TEAM. YOU EITHER GET BETTER PLAYERS OR GET THE PLAYERS YOU'VE GOT TO PLAY BETTER.

Bum Phillips
Houston Oilers

36

THERE WILL BE TWO BUSSES LEAVING THE HOTEL FOR TOMORROW NIGHT'S GAME. THE 2:00 PM BUS WILL BE FOR THOSE OF YOU WHO NEED A LITTLE EXTRA WORK. THE EMPTY BUS WILL LEAVE AT 5:00 PM.

Dave Bristol
San Francisco Giants

I'M NOT THE MANAGER BECAUSE I'M ALWAYS RIGHT, BUT I'M ALWAYS RIGHT BECAUSE I'M THE MANAGER.

Gene Mauch
California Angels

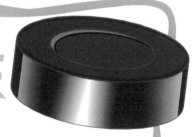

I KNOW MY PLAYERS DON'T LIKE MY PRACTICES, BUT THEN, I DON'T LIKE THEIR GAMES.

Harry Neale
Vancouver Canucks
During a losing streak.

39

THE TOUGHEST THING FOR ME AS A YOUNG MANAGER IS THAT A LOT OF MY PLAYERS SAW ME PLAY. THEY KNOW HOW BAD I WAS.

Tony La Russa
Oakland Athletics

I GIVE THE SAME HALF-TIME SPEECH OVER AND OVER. IT WORKS BEST WHEN MY PLAYERS ARE BETTER THAN THE OTHER COACH'S PLAYERS.

Chuck Mills
Wake Forest Football

41

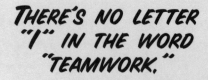

*THERE'S NO LETTER
"I" IN THE WORD
"TEAMWORK."*

Bill Foster
Virginia Tech University Basketball

42

MANAGING IS LIKE HOLDING A DOVE IN YOUR HAND. SQUEEZE TOO HARD AND YOU KILL IT, NOT ENOUGH AND IT FLIES AWAY.

Tommy Lasorda
Los Angeles Dodgers

I'VE LEARNED THAT THE ONLY WAY TO GET RESPECT FROM PEOPLE IS TO GIVE THEM RESPECT. AND THAT'S MY WAY OF DOING IT.

Tommy Lasorda
Los Angeles Dodgers

43

Character

The great coaches are defined by their strength of character. The will of the coach is the backbone of the team, and if the moral or ethical structure of the coach is in question, the team is likely to lack discipline and dedication to the team. The champions who benefitted under the tutelage of the following coaches did so because of the solid foundation their coaches provided.

BE A DREAMER.
IF YOU DON'T KNOW
HOW TO DREAM,
YOU'RE DEAD.

Jim Valvano
North Carolina State University Basketball

I'LL SAY THIS. THIS IS THE GREATEST BALL CLUB A MAN COULD MANAGE. CERTAINLY THE BEST I'VE EVER KNOWN. I AM INDEBTED TO THEM FOR THE WAY THEY CAME THROUGH FOR ME. THEY WON IT, NOT ME.

Casey Stengel
New York Yankees
Reflecting on his New York Yankees.

46

ANYONE WHO WILL TEAR DOWN SPORTS WILL TEAR DOWN AMERICA. SPORTS AND RELIGION HAVE MADE AMERICA WHAT IT IS TODAY.

Woody Hayes
Ohio State University Football

*THE REAL GLORY IS BEING KNOCKED TO
YOUR KNEES AND THEN COMING BACK.
THAT'S REAL GLORY. THAT'S THE ESSENCE OF IT.*

Vince Lombardi
Green Bay Packers

*THE ACHIEVEMENTS OF AN ORGANIZATION
ARE THE RESULT OF THE COMBINED EFFORT
OF EACH INDIVIDUAL.*

Vince Lombardi
Green Bay Packers

IT'S NOT WHETHER YOU GET KNOCKED DOWN.
IT'S WHETHER YOU GET UP AGAIN.

Vince Lombardi
Green Bay Packers

THE GREATEST ACCOMPLISHMENT
IS NOT IN NEVER FALLING,
BUT IN RISING AGAIN
AFTER YOU FALL.

Vince Lombardi
Green Bay Packers

49

THE WHEEZE ABOUT BUILDING CHARACTER IS A JOKE. MOST BOYS WE GET ARE 18. THEIR CHARACTER HAS LONG SINCE BEEN BUILT, USUALLY IN THE HOME. ABOUT ALL WE CAN TEACH A KID IS HOW TO PLAY FOOTBALL.

John McKay
USC Football

THE WILL TO WIN IS IMPORTANT, BUT THE WILL TO PREPARE IS VITAL.

Joe Paterno
Pennsylvania State University Football

I DON'T WANT ANY HOT DOGS ON MY TEAM. IF YOU'RE A HOT DOG, YOU TEND TO GET CARELESS IN THE GAME.

Joe Paterno
University of Pennsylvania Football

I HAD NO PARTICULAR AMBITIONS AS A CHILD OTHER THAN BEING A BASEBALL PLAYER. IT WASN'T UNTIL I WAS A SOPHOMORE AT CRANE TECH HIGH SCHOOL THAT I RECOGNIZED THAT I'D NEVER BE A GENIUS AND THAT TO GET ANYWHERE, I WOULD HAVE TO WORK HARD. I'VE BEEN WORKING HARD EVER SINCE.

George Halas
Chicago Bears

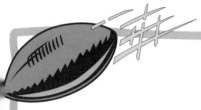

I DON'T THINK ANYTHING IS UNREALISTIC IF YOU BELIEVE YOU CAN DO IT. I THINK IF YOU ARE DETERMINED ENOUGH AND WILLING TO PAY THE PRICE, YOU CAN GET IT DONE.

Mike Ditka
Chicago Bears

FOOTBALL ISN'T MEANT TO BE PLAYED FOR MONEY.

Bob Zuppke
University of Illinois

54

WHAT YOU LACK IN TALENT CAN BE MADE UP WITH DESIRE, HUSTLE AND GIVING 110 PERCENT ALL THE TIME.

Don Zimmer
Chicago Cubs

55

I RESPECT COLLEGE COACHES WHO RAISE KIDS THE RIGHT WAY, WHO WON'T ALLOW THEIR KIDS TO GO OUT LOOKING FOR A FIGHT, TAUNTING, GYRATING. TAUNTING AND GYRATING? I DON'T LIKE COACHES WHO ALLOW THAT. I MIGHT BE AN ASS MYSELF, BUT MY PLAYERS ARE NOT PERMITTED. THEY REPRESENT SO MUCH MORE THAN JUST BASKETBALL. IF I EVER SAW ONE OF MY KIDS DOING THAT, I'D TAKE HIM OUT. I HAVE SOME BAD KIDS SOMETIMES, SOME STINKERS LIKE ANYBODY ELSE. BUT THE GUY WHO'S A STINKER WON'T BE AROUND LONG. I'M CONCERNED WITH THE LARGER ISSUE OF HOW COACHES RAISE THEIR PLAYERS TO PLAY THIS GAME... COACHES—WE

DON'T TEACH ANY DAMN CLASS. ALL WE'VE GOT TO DO IS DEVELOP CHARACTER. YOU'VE GOT 11, 12, 13 KIDS HARNESSED AND YOU CANNOT CONTROL THE TAUNTING? THAT, TO ME, IS INEXCUSABLE. MANY OF US IN THIS BUSINESS ARE FOLLOWING SOME OTHER KIND OF MUSIC. TO HAVE DISCIPLINE AND DIRECTION FOR OUR KIDS... WE ARE THE LAST CHANCE AT IT. CHARACTER IS THE THING THEY BETTER HAVE.

John Chaney
Temple University Basketball

57

PUSH YOURSELF AGAIN AND AGAIN.
DON'T GIVE AN INCH UNTIL
THE FINAL BUZZER SOUNDS.

Larry Bird
Indiana Pacers

LEAVE AS LITTLE CHANCE AS POSSIBLE. PREPARATION IS THE KEY TO SUCCESS.

Paul Brown
Cleveland Browns

OUR THEME HAS BEEN THAT HARD WORK EQUALS SUCCESS. WE HAVEN'T DONE IT WITH MAGIC OR WITH BETTER PLAYS OR ANYTHING LIKE THAT.

Don Shula
Miami Dolphins

I THINK IT'S PART OF AMERICANA THAT YOU MAKE SACRIFICES TO PLAY IT. YOU HAVE 11 GUYS AND ONE BALL. THE 11 ON DEFENSE HAVE THE OBJECTIVE TO GET THE BALL. THE KIND OF SACRIFICES YOU HAVE TO MAKE TO BE A GUARD OR A TACKLE OR A DEFENSIVE NOSE TACKLE, I THINK MOST PEOPLE CAN PROBABLY RELATE TO THAT.

Dennis Green
Minnesota Vikings
Talking about football.

61

*HE WAS HUSTLING,
AND GOOD THINGS HAPPEN
TO PEOPLE WHO HUSTLE.*

Chuck Noll
Pittsburgh Steelers
Referring to a Franco Harris touchdown
reception.

I TRY FOR GOOD PLAYERS AND I TRY FOR GOOD CHARACTER. IF NECESSARY, THOUGH, I SETTLE FOR THE GOOD PLAYER.

Phil Maloney
Vancouver Canucks

63

*TURN YOUR LOSSES INTO A PLUS.
I THINK IF YOU APPROACH IT RIGHT, YOU
CAN TURN EVERY SETBACK YOU HAVE INTO
AN ADVANTAGE.*

George Allen
Washington Redskins

I'VE GOT FAR LESS PATIENCE WITH TALENTED PLAYERS WHO MALINGER. TO ME, THE STOMACH (A PLAYER'S GUTS AND HEART) IS FAR MORE IMPORTANT THAN THE ARMS AND LEGS. GIVE ME AN AVERAGE PLAYER WITH A GOOD STOMACH AND I'LL TAKE HIM OVER A GUY WITH SUPER ABILITY IN MOST INSTANCES. WHEN WE SCOUT, WE'RE TOOL PEOPLE—STRONG ARMS, LEGS, POWER. BUT THE MORE YOU MANAGE, YOU REALIZE IT'S NOT THE TOOLS THAT BEAT YOU. IT'S THE GUY WHO'S NOT AFRAID TO BE UP THERE WHEN THE GAME'S ON THE LINE.

Buck Rodgers
California Angels

65

ABILITY MAY GET YOU TO THE TOP, BUT IT TAKES CHARACTER TO KEEP YOU THERE.

John Wooden
UCLA Basketball

CLASS IS AN INTANGIBLE QUALITY WHICH COMMANDS, RATHER THAN DEMANDS, THE RESPECT OF OTHERS.

John Wooden
UCLA Basketball

66

THE ONLY DISCIPLINE THAT LASTS IS SELF-DISCIPLINE.

Bum Phillips
Houston Oilers

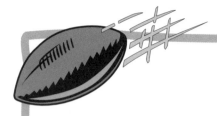

If ONE LESS PERSON HAD PUT OUT ONE LESS PERCENT WE WOULD HAVE LOST.

Tommy Prothro
UCLA Football
His reaction to UCLA's upset of Michigan State
in the 1966 Rose Bowl.

68

> *AS LONG AS A PERSON DOESN'T ADMIT HE IS DEFEATED, HE IS NOT DEFEATED – HE'S JUST A LITTLE BEHIND AND ISN'T THROUGH FIGHTING.*

Darrell Royal
University of Texas Football

> *FOOTBALL DOESN'T BUILD CHARACTER. IT ELIMINATES THE WEAK ONES.*

Darrell Royal
University of Texas Football

69

Winning

Any coach will tell you all he cares about is winning. This singular sense of purpose gives the team a course to follow on the road to a championship. Nowhere is this reflected more accurately than in the minds and words of the following coaches.

WHEN I STARTED, I'D WALK THE STREETS ALL NIGHT AFTER A LOSS. I COULDN'T EAT OR SLEEP. AS THE YEARS WENT BY, I CAME TO REALIZE LOSING IS AS MUCH A PART OF COACHING AS WINNING. THE GAME IS A SLICE OF LIFE. THERE IS GOOD IN EVERY EXPERIENCE IF YOU LEARN FROM IT.

Ray Meyer
DePaul Basketball

71

*THEY SAY I TEACH BRUTAL FOOTBALL.
THE ONLY THING BRUTAL ABOUT FOOTBALL
IS LOSING.*

Paul "Bear" Bryant
University of Alabama Football

*SHOW CLASS, HAVE PRIDE AND DISPLAY
CHARACTER. IF YOU DO, WINNING TAKES
CARE OF ITSELF.*

Paul "Bear" Bryant
University of Alabama Football

WINNING ISN'T EVERYTHING, BUT IT BEATS ANYTHING THAT COMES IN SECOND.

Paul "Bear" Bryant
*University of
Alabama Football*

JUST ONCE I'D LIKE TO SEE THE
WIN-LOSS RECORDS OF DOCTORS
RIGHT OUT FRONT WHERE PEOPLE
COULD SEE THEM - WON TEN,
LOST THREE, TIED TWO.

Abe Lemons
University of Texas Basketball

14

IT'S EASY TO HAVE FAITH IN YOURSELF AND HAVE DISCIPLINE WHEN YOU'RE A WINNER, WHEN YOU'RE NUMBER ONE. WHAT YOU GOT TO HAVE IS FAITH AND DISIPLINE WHEN YOU'RE NOT A WINNER.

Vince Lombardi
Green Bay Packers

THE SPIRIT, THE WILL TO WIN, AND THE WILL TO EXCEL ARE THE THINGS THAT ENDURE. THESE QUALITIES ARE SO MUCH MORE IMPORTANT THAN THE EVENTS THAT OCCUR.

Vince Lombardi
Green Bay Packers

WIN THIS ONE FOR THE GIPPER.

Knute Rockne
Notre Dame Football

SHOW ME A GOOD AND GRACIOUS LOSER, AND I'LL SHOW YOU A FAILURE.

Knute Rockne
Notre Dame Football

KNUTE ROCKNE WANTED NOTHING BUT "BAD LOSERS." GOOD LOSERS GET INTO THE HABIT OF LOSING.

George Allen
Washington Redskins

EVERY TIME YOU WIN YOU'RE REBORN; WHEN YOU LOSE, YOU DIE A LITTLE.

George Allen
Washington Redskins

IF WE REALLY WANT TO PUT ACADEMICS FIRST, WE HAVE TO LET FRESHMEN SPEND THEIR FIRST YEAR WITHOUT PRESSURE AND FREE TO STUDY. I THINK IT WOULD BE ALL RIGHT TO LET THEM PRACTICE THREE DAYS A WEEK TO KEEP THEIR GAME SHARP, BUT I HAVE SEEN THE PRESSURE FRESHMEN ARE UNDER AND I THINK IT IS HARMFUL...BUT THE MEDIA IS LOOKING FOR A MESSIAH. IT IS LOOKING FOR A NEW MICHAEL JORDAN OR LARRY BIRD OR MAGIC JOHNSON. IT JUST NEVER LETS UP.

Lou Campanelli
University of California, Berkeley Basketball

78

A WINNER IS SOMEONE WHO RECOGNIZES HIS GOD-GIVEN TALENTS, WORKS HIS TAIL OFF TO DEVELOP THEM INTO SKILLS, AND USES THESE SKILLS TO ACCOMPLISH HIS GOALS.

Larry Bird
Indiana Pacers

YOU HAVE TO KNOW SOMETHING ABOUT THESE PLAYERS. SOMETIME BACK IN THE SEVENTH OR THE EIGHTH GRADE, THEY WERE CALLED OUT OF LINE AND DESIGNATED AS SPECIAL. WHY? BECAUSE THEY WERE A LITTLE BETTER AT BASKETBALL THAN THE NEXT KID. THEY STARTED GETTING SPECIAL TREATMENT. AND IT HAS NEVER CHANGED. ALL THEY HAVE EVER KNOWN IS SPECIAL TREATMENT. YOU CANNOT BE TOO DEMANDING. AT THIS LEVEL,

THERE HAS GOT TO BE CONSTANT GIVE-AND-TAKE. YOU TAKE THE ASSETS YOU HAVE AND PUT THEM IN A SYSTEM THAT WORKS, OFFENSIVELY AND DEFENSIVELY. AND IF YOU'RE LUCKY, IF YOU CAN SELL THEM ON ALL THAT, SOMETIMES YOU CAN BUILD SOMETHING TOGETHER THAT LASTS.

Chuck Daly
New Jersey Nets

81

FAILURES ARE EXPECTED BY LOSERS, IGNORED BY WINNERS.

Joe Gibbs
Washington Redskins

82

WINNING IS THE EPITOME OF HONESTY ITSELF.

Woody Hayes
Ohio State University Football

When you're a winner, you come back no matter what happened the day before.

Billy Martin
New York Yankees

The idea in this game isn't to win popularity polls or to be a good guy to everyone. The name of the game is win.

Billy Martin
New York Yankees

IF THERE IS SUCH A GOOD THING AS A GOOD LOSER, THEN THE GAME IS CROOKED.

Billy Martin
New York Yankees

85

WINNING AND LOSING
ARE BOTH VERY TEMPORARY THINGS.
HAVING DONE ONE OR THE OTHER,
YOU MOVE AHEAD.

Chuck Knox
Los Angeles Rams

NICE GUYS FINISH LAST.

Leo Durocher
Chicago Cubs

*HOW YOU PLAY THE GAME IS FOR
COLLEGE BOYS. WHEN YOU'RE PLAYING
FOR MONEY, WINNING IS THE ONLY
THING THAT COUNTS.*

Leo Durocher
Chicago Cubs

87

SHOW ME A GOOD LOSER
AND I'LL SHOW YOU A LOSER.

Arnold "Red" Auerbach

88

IT AIN'T OVER TIL IT'S OVER.

Yogi Berra
New York Yankees

89

If I had had the attitude that I had to play every day to be happy, I wouldn't be here right now...
I'd rather be a swing man on a championship team than a regular on another team.

Lou Piniella
Seattle Mariners

YOU MUST WIN, BUT YOU ALSO MUST HAVE FUN OR WHAT'S THE USE? FOOTBALL IS BUT A SMALL PART OF ALL OF OUR LIVES.

Bum Phillips
Houston Oilers

WINNING IS THE NAME OF THE GAME. THE BOTTOM LINE IS WE NEED TO FINISH PLAYS.

Buddy Ryan
Arizona Cardinals

THEY NEVER GIVE UP.

Bengt Ohlson
Sweden National Hockey
Talking about the U.S. Hockey Team.

93

COLLEGE BASKETBALL HAS BECOME A MORE UNFORGIVING BUSINESS IN RECENT YEARS. I THINK SOME OF IT HAS DRIFTED DOWN FROM THE NBA. THE EXTERNAL INFLUENCES ON KIDS ARE FAR GREATER THAN 10 YEARS AGO. A LOT OF KIDS FIND IT DIFFICULT TO TRANSLATE INDIVIDUAL ACHIEVEMENT INTO TEAM BASKETBALL. I THINK THE ULTIMATE WAS IN 1991, WHEN BOTH DUKE AND NORTH CAROLINA WENT TO THE FINAL FOUR AND EACH TEAM LOST TWO KIDS BECAUSE THEY DIDN'T PLAY ENOUGH.

Ernie Nestor
George Mason University Basketball

PEOPLE LIKE TO TELL YOU THAT THEY CAN LEAVE THE GAME AT THE BALLPARK. I TRY TO DO THAT, BUT I CAN'T. I TRY TO HIDE IT. EVERYBODY AROUND ME WILL THINK I'M NOT THINKING ABOUT BASEBALL; EXCEPT MY FAMILY—THEY KNOW WHEN SOMETHING IS BOTHERING ME. MY WIFE SAYS SHE KNOWS THE MINUTE I COME OUT OF THE CLUBHOUSE WHAT THE NIGHT WILL BE LIKE. SHE DOESN'T EVEN HAVE TO SAY, "HELLO, HOW ARE YOU DOING?" SHE JUST LOOKS AT ME, AND SHE KNOWS.

Johnny Oates
Baltimore Orioles

95

WHEN I WAS COACHING THE LOS ANGELES LAKERS, THE BOSTON CELTICS WOULD BEAT US AND WE'D PAT THEM ON THE BACK AND SAY, "GREAT GAME, GREAT SERIES." THAT'S B.S. YOU CAN'T WIN WORRYING ABOUT WHETHER PEOPLE LIKE YOU. YOU JUST CAN'T.

Pat Riley
Los Angeles Lakers
Talking after he'd left the team to become
head coach of the New York Knicks.

96

THE ONLY YARDSTICK FOR SUCCESS OUR SOCIETY HAS IS BEING A CHAMPION. NO ONE REMEMBERS ANYTHING ELSE.

John Madden
Oakland Raiders

97

A WINNER NEVER WHINES.

Paul Brown
Cleveland Browns

WHEN WE LOSE I CAN'T SLEEP AT NIGHT. WHEN WE WIN I CAN'T SLEEP AT NIGHT, BUT WHEN YOU WIN, YOU WAKE UP FEELING BETTER.

Joe Torre
New York Yankees

On the Job

Coaching is a rewarding and satisfying job. But it is not without daily pressure and rigorous demands. Life in this "fishbowl environment" is filled with ups and downs, and this section gives us a slice of their lives.

THE COMPETITION IN THE JOB MARKET
TODAY CALLS FOR BEING AS WELL-
PREPARED AS POSSIBLE. YOU MUST
PREPARE FOR YOUR FUTURE, AND THAT
KEY IS EDUCATION.

Paul "Bear" Bryant
University of Alabama Football

I FEEL LIKE A GUY IN AN OPEN CASKET AT HIS OWN FUNERAL. EVERYONE WALKS BY AND SAYS WHAT A GOOD GUY YOU WERE. BUT IT DOESN'T DO YOU ANY GOOD. YOU'RE STILL DEAD.

Tom Trebelhorn
Milwaukee Brewers
On his firing.

*THERE ARE TWO TYPES OF COACHES.
THEM THAT HAVE JUST BEEN FIRED,
AND THEM THAT ARE GOING TO BE FIRED.*

Bum Phillips
Houston Oilers

IF YOU AREN'T FIRED WITH ENTHUSIASM, YOU WILL BE FIRED WITH ENTHUSIASM.

Vince Lombardi
Green Bay Packers

THE SECRET OF MANAGING IS TO KEEP THE GUYS WHO HATE YOU AWAY FROM THE GUYS THAT ARE UNDECIDED.

Casey Stengel
New York Yankees

MANAGING IS GETTING PAID FOR HOME RUNS SOMEONE ELSE HITS.

Casey Stengel
New York Yankees

105

I DISCOVERED *I* COULD BE FAR MORE EFFECTIVE AS A COACH WHEN *I* BALANCED THE MASCULINE AND FEMININE SIDES OF MY NATURE.

Phil Jackson
Chicago Bulls

106

IT WAS NOT UNTIL I MANAGED MY FIRST GAME THAT I REALIZED THE RESPONSIBILITY THAT GOES WITH BEING A BLACK MANAGER. AS A MINORITY, I HAVE TO BE A GOOD EXAMPLE. THOSE OF US (MINORITY MANAGERS) WHO ARE IN EMINENCE NOW HAVE TO SHOW PEOPLE THAT WE ARE CAPABLE OF CONTROLLING A GAME, HANDLING PLAYERS AND THE MEDIA, AND CAN HAVE A GOOD RELATIONSHIP WITH THE FANS AND THE CITY IN WHICH WE MANAGE. IF WE DON'T MANAGE WELL OR MIX WELL WITH THE FANS, THE NEXT MINORITY GUY ISN'T GOING TO HAVE MUCH OF A CHANCE.

Felipe Alou
Montreal Expos

A BASEBALL MANAGER IS A NECESSARY EVIL.

Sparky Anderson
Cincinnati Reds

I DON'T THINK YOU MANAGE A TEAM TODAY UNLESS YOU TRULY RESPECT THE PLAYERS. I RESPECT PLAYERS ON ALL TEAMS... IT LOOKS EASY AND WONDERFUL TO BE A PLAYER, BUT THEY'RE AWAY FROM THEIR FAMILIES ALL THE TIME, TRAVELLING AND TAKING ABUSE FROM THE FANS. THEY'RE PUT ON A PEDESTAL AND EXPECTED TO BE LIKE GOD, AND THEY'RE NOT. THEY'RE HUMAN BEINGS WHO MAKE MISTAKES LIKE EVERYBODY ELSE. I REALLY RESPECT HOW THEY GO ABOUT THEIR WORK.

Sparky Anderson
Cincinnati Reds

I THINK THAT MY WHOLE SECRET AS A MANAGER HAS BEEN I WAS NEVER AFRAID TO LOSE MY JOB. I TELL OTHER MANAGERS, "DON'T EVEN THINK ABOUT THAT'S GOING ON UPSTAIRS (WITH THE OWNER)." YOU CAN'T STOP THEM IF THEY WANT TO FIRE YOU. JUST DO THE BEST JOB YOU CAN. IF YOU'RE A MANAGER, THERE'S NO DISGRACE TO BEING FIRED. MANAGERS ARE FIRED ALL THE TIME. BUT IT IS A DISGRACE TO SELL YOUR HONOR.

Sparky Anderson
Cincinnati Reds

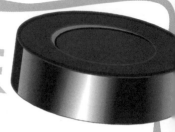

WITH THE CHANGE IN SOCIETY, YOU NATURALLY HAVE A DIFFERENT BRAND OF PLAYER TODAY. YOU USED TO TELL A PLAYER SOMETHING, AND HE WOULD DO IT WITH NO QUESTIONS ASKED BECAUSE HE WAS SCARED TO DEATH OF LOSING HIS JOB. THE PLAYERS RUN THE GAME NOW, AND MONEY HAS MADE THE GAME A BUSINESS. NOW, WHEN A COACH TELLS A PLAYER TO DO SOMETHING, HE WANTS TO KNOW WHY.

110

Al Arbour
New York Islanders

PLAYERS KNOW WHO'S THE MANAGER. THEY KNOW WHO'S THE BOSS. THEY KNOW I'M THE BOSS. THEY KNOW WHEN I'M JOKING AND WHEN I'M SERIOUS. I OPERATE ON A STERN DISCIPLINE AND UNDERSTANDING. I DON'T TOLERATE A LACK OF EFFORT. I STILL REALIZE HOW HARD THE GAME IS. IT'S HARD. SOME OF THESE GUYS MAKE IT LOOK EASY, BUT IT NEVER REALLY IS.

Dusty Baker
San Francisco Giants

WHAT YOU SAY IN A LOCKER ROOM SHOULD BE BETWEEN THE COACH AND THE PLAYERS. NO ONE ELSE'S BUSINESS. I MAY HAVE USED SOME CURSE WORDS. BUT FROM GEORGE RAVELING TO BOBBY KNIGHT TO DEAN SMITH, THERE'S NOT A COACH IN THE COUNTRY THAT DOESN'T.

Lou Campanelli
University of California, Berkeley Basketball
Speaking about being fired because of
post-game tirades in the locker-room.

THEY'LL FIRE YOU FOR LOSING BEFORE THEY FIRE YOU FOR CHEATING.

Darrell Royal
University of Texas Football

JUST GIVE EVERY COACH THE SAME AMOUNT OF MONEY AND TELL HIM HE CAN KEEP WHAT'S LEFT OVER.

Abe Lemmons
University of Texas Basketball
On how to solve recruiting violations.

I'D RATHER BE A FOOTBALL COACH. THAT WAY YOU ONLY LOSE 11 GAMES A YEAR.

Abe Lemmons
University of Texas Basketball

114

IF YOU DON'T WIN, YOU'RE GOING TO GET FIRED. IF YOU DO WIN, YOU'VE ONLY PUT OFF THE DAY YOU'RE GOING TO BE FIRED.

Leo Durocher
Chicago Cubs

115

BEHIND EVERY FIRED COLLEGE FOOTBALL COACH STANDS A COLLEGE PRESIDENT.

John McKay
USC Football

I'M NOT SURE WHETHER I'D BE MANAGING OR TESTING BULLETPROOF VESTS.

Joe Torre
New York Yankees
Talking about a possible life without baseball.

17

THE 45 SECOND CLOCK HAS TAKEN SOMETHING AWAY FROM ME. I'M NOT AS GOOD A COACH AS I WAS BEFORE THE CLOCK AND THE THREE POINT SHOT. WHEN WE GOT AHEAD BEFORE THE CLOCK, WE DIDN'T LOSE. IT WAS MORE OF A COACHES' GAME THEN THAN IT IS NOW. WHAT WE HAVE NOW IS A FAN'S THING, AND I'M NOT SAYING THAT IS GOOD OR BAD.

Bobby Knight
University of Indiana Basketball

I'LL SEE A KID, AND I SAY TO MYSELF, "THAT KID CAN'T PLAY FOR ME." WELL, THAT SIMPLY MEANS ONE THING: THE KID CAN'T PLAY FOR ME. THAT DOESN'T MEAN THAT HE'S A BAD PLAYER OR THAT HE'S A BAD KID. HE MAY BE A HELL OF A PLAYER AND HE MAY BE THE BEST KID POSSIBLE, BUT HE HAS A WAY OF PLAYING THAT ISN'T GOING TO FIT INTO WHAT I WANT TO DO. THEN, I ALSO HAVE TO THINK TO MYSELF THAT IT ISN'T JUST THAT THAT KID CAN'T PLAY FOR ME, BUT FROM THAT KID'S STANDPOINT, I'M NOT THE COACH FOR HIM.

Bobby Knight
University of Indiana Basketball

Why can't hockey coaches be in the job as long as NFL coaches? Why can't this happen? Basketball and football coaches are sometimes around 15 or 20 years. We're very quick to pull the trigger on coaches in the NHL, it seems. You have 20 people in front of you. All are young guys compared to other sports and you've got to get them all on page one. It takes time.

Terry Murray
Washington Capitals

120

YOU KNOW ON THE FRONT END THAT THIS IS PART OF THE BUSINESS. IT'S BECOME A MORE UNFORTUNATE BUSINESS IN RECENT YEARS AND THE EXTERNAL INFLUENCES ON THE KIDS ARE FAR GREATER THAN 10 YEARS AGO. IT'S MORE DIFFICULT TO TRANSLATE INDIVIDUAL ACHIEVEMENT INTO TEAM BASKETBALL. THIS IS A JOB OF HIGHS AND LOWS, WITH NOT A LOT IN THE MIDDLE. YOU'RE JUDGED ON SUCCESS, AND WE HAVEN'T HAD A LOT IN THE LAST TWO YEARS.

Ernie Nestor
*George Mason University Basketball
Talking about his being forced to resign his position as head coach.*

WE'VE GOT A SCREWED UP SYSTEM IN BASEBALL RIGHT NOW. IT'S TOUGH TO DIFFERENTIATE RIGHT FROM WRONG. WE'RE REWARDING GUYS FOR HITTING .220. I MEAN, WE OFFERED A THREE-YEAR CONTRACT TO DICK SCHOFIELD FOR $6.5 MILLION. AND HE'S DUMBER THAN WE ARE. HE TURNED IT DOWN. IT'S LIKE WE'RE TRYING TO OUT-DUMB EACH OTHER. THEY ASKED ME, "WHAT WOULD YOU DO ABOUT SCHOFIELD?" I SAID, "I'D RELEASE THE GUY. IF YOU CAN'T FIND A GUY WHO CAN HIT .220, THERE'S SOMETHING WRONG WITH THIS GAME."

122

Buck Rodgers
California Angels

PLAYER FIGHTING IS PART OF HOCKEY. I FEEL
IN 10 YEARS THAT FIGHTING WILL BE ELIMINATED IN THE
NHL. IN THE MEANTIME, IF FIGHTING IS PART OF THE
GAME, YOU'VE GOT TO HAVE PEOPLE TO GO OUT THERE AND
STAND UP FOR THEIR TEAMMATES. I'M NOT PARTICULARLY
IN FAVOR OF FIGHTING FOR FIGHTING'S SAKE, BUT IF A
TEAM IS GETTING CARRIED AWAY, YOU HAVE TO HAVE
PEOPLE TO RESPOND.

Ron Wilson
Anaheim Mighty Ducks

123

I HAD A FRIEND WITH A LIFETIME CONTRACT. AFTER TWO BAD YEARS THE UNIVERSITY PRESIDENT CALLED HIM INTO HIS OFFICE AND PRONOUNCED HIM DEAD.

Bob Devaney
University of Nebraska Football

COACHING IS NOTHING MORE THAN ELIMINATING MISTAKES BEFORE YOU GET FIRED.

Lou Holtz
Notre Dame Football

125

PEOPLE WHO ENJOY WHAT THEY ARE DOING INVARIABLY DO IT WELL.

Joe Gibbs
Washington Redskins

IF YOU'RE A PRO COACH, "NFL" STANDS FOR "NOT FOR LONG."

Jerry Glanville
Atlanta Falcons

WHEN YOU'RE A COACH, YOU'RE MISERABLE. WHEN YOU'RE NOT A COACH, YOU'RE MORE MISERABLE.

Fred Shero
Philadelphia Flyers

FOOTBALL DOESN'T TAKE ME AWAY FROM MY FAMILY LIFE. WE'VE ALWAYS WATCHED FILMS TOGETHER.

Fred Akers
University of Texas Football

IF YOU START WORRYING ABOUT THE PEOPLE IN THE STANDS, BEFORE TOO LONG YOU'RE IN THE STANDS WITH THEM.

Tommy Lasorda
Los Angeles Dodgers

I FOUND OUT THAT IT'S NOT GOOD TO TALK ABOUT MY TROUBLES. EIGHTY PERCENT OF THE PEOPLE WHO HEAR THEM DON'T CARE AND THE OTHER TWENTY PERCENT ARE GLAD YOU'RE HAVING TROUBLE.

Tom Lasorda
Los Angeles Dodgers

WHEN THE ATHLETIC DIRECTOR SAID I SHOULD RECRUIT MORE WHITE PLAYERS TO KEEP THE FOLKS IN PULLMAN HAPPY, I SIGNED RUFUS WHITE AND WILLIE WHITE.

George Raveling
Washington State Basketball

131

ANY KID WHO WOULD LEAVE THAT WONDERFUL WEATHER IS TOO DUMB TO PLAY FOR US.

Alex Agase
Purdue University Football
On why he doesn't try to get Californians.

I HAD ONE REAL GOOD ONE IN FLORIDA TO RECRUIT. I REALLY WORKED ON THE PARENTS, BELIEVING IT TO BE THE WAY. COACH BEAR BRYANT OF ALABAMA WORKED ON THE BOY. I DINED AND DANCED WITH THE BOY'S MOTHER. THE BOY WENT TO ALABAMA. THE MOTHER ENROLLED AT MIAMI.

Otis Mooney
Miami University Football

133

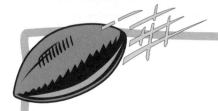

NOBODY SHOULD WORK ALL THE TIME.
EVERYONE SHOULD HAVE SOME LEISURE.
I BELIEVE THE EARLY MORNING HOURS
ARE BEST FOR THIS—THE FIVE OR SIX
HOURS WHEN YOU'RE ASLEEP.

George Allen
Washington Redskins

Etc.

A strong and distinct personality are almost a prerequisite for a coach. This next section gives us a sampling of the diversity and color of some of our best known and loved coaches.

I WAS GLAD IT WAS HIS HEAD
AND NOT HIS KNEE.

Tom Landry
Dallas Cowboys
On an injury to Roger Staubach.

I WON'T KNOW UNTIL MY BARBER TELLS ME ON MONDAY.

Knute Rockne
Notre Dame Football
His response to a question on why his team had just lost.

FOOTBALL IS A GAME PLAYED WITH THE ARMS, LEGS AND SHOULDERS, BUT MOSTLY FROM THE NECK UP.

Knute Rockne
Notre Dame Football

IF YOU BURN YOUR NEIGHBOR'S HOUSE, IT DOESN'T MAKE YOUR HOME LOOK BETTER.

Lou Holtz
Notre Dame Football

I DON'T MIND STARTING A SEASON WITH UNKNOWNS. I JUST DON'T LIKE FINISHING A SEASON WITH A BUNCH OF THEM.

Lou Holtz
Notre Dame Football

*IF I EVER NEED A BRAIN TRANSPLANT,
I WANT ONE FROM A SPORTSWRITER,
BECAUSE I'LL KNOW IT'S NEVER BEEN USED.*

Joe Paterno
Pennsylvania State University Football

LOOK AT THAT GUY. CAN'T HIT, CAN'T RUN, CAN'T CATCH. OF COURSE, THAT'S WHY THEY GAVE HIM TO US.

Casey Stengel
New York Yankees

GOOD PITCHING WILL ALWAYS STOP GOOD HITTING, AND VICE VERSA.

Casey Stengel
New York Yankees

BEING WITH A WOMAN ALL NIGHT NEVER HURT NO PROFESSIONAL BASEBALL PLAYER. IT'S THE STAYING UP ALL NIGHT LOOKING FOR ONE THAT DOES HIM IN.

Casey Stengel
New York Yankees

THERE ARE THINGS KIDS DO IN THE CITY THAT THEY DON'T DO ANYWHERE ELSE. WE LOVE COURT SAVVY. YOU DON'T TEACH IT; YOU GET IT IN THE CITY. NEW YORK KIDS HAVE COURT SAVVY.

Dean Smith
University of North Carolina Basketball

142

FUNDAMENTALS ARE LACKING IN ALL COLLEGE SPORTS NOW, NOT ONLY BASEBALL BUT BASKETBALL AND FOOTBALL. EVERYBODY TODAY IS A STAR, AND IT'S VERY DIFFICULT TO TEACH THEM. SOME OF IT IS LACK OF SELF-DISCIPLINE. BASEBALL IS A GAME OF CONCENTRATION. YOU MAY STAND IN RIGHT FIELD FOR FIVE INNINGS WITH NOTHING TO DO, BUT YOU'D BETTER BE READY WHEN SOMETHING COMES YOUR WAY.

Joe Duff
U.S. Naval Academy Baseball

143

IT'S NEVER AS GOOD AS YOU THINK IT IS, AND IT IS NEVER AS BAD AS YOU THINK IT IS.

Rich Kotite
Philadelphia Eagles

THE GAME COMBINES SO MANY OF THE BEST ASPECTS OF OTHER SPORTS AND ELIMINATES SOME OF THE BAD ONES. IT HAS THE SPEED OF HOCKEY, BUT WITHOUT THE FIGHTING. IT HAS THE TEAMWORK OF SOCCER, BUT WITH MORE SCORING. PEOPLE ARE DRAWN TO THE CONTINUOUS ACTION, TO THE SPEED OF THE GAME AND TO THE PHYSICAL CONTACT. IT HAS A LITTLE OF EVERYTHING AND YET THERE'S NO NEED FOR A 300 POUND LINEMAN OR A SEVEN-FOOT CENTER. THERE ARE NO PHYSICAL PREJUDICES.

Dick Edell
University of Maryland Lacrosse

IN BASEBALL, YOU DON'T KNOW NOTHING.

Yogi Berra
New York Yankees

IF THE PEOPLE DON'T WANT TO COME OUT TO THE PARK, NOBODY'S GOING TO STOP THEM.

Yogi Berra
New York Yankees

HE WAS A HARD OUT.

Yogi Berra
New York Yankees
Talking about Jackie Robinson.

IT'S NOT OVER UNTIL IT'S OVER.

Yogi Berra
New York Yankees

I DON'T HAVE ANY EXPERTISE IN UNIFORMS. I THINK ALL UNIFORMS LOOK NICE IF YOU'VE GOT GOOD PLAYERS IN THEM.

Bill Parcells
New England Patriots
Talking about his team's new uniforms.

WE HAVE A RULE THAT OUR BACKS DON'T FUMBLE, BECAUSE IF THEY DO THEY WILL BE IN SOMEONE ELSE'S BACKFIELD.

Bill Parcells
New York Giants

TIMES HAVE NOT CHANGED. FOOTBALL HAS NOT CHANGED. IT DOES NOT CHANGE. IT EVOLVES SOME, CERTAINLY, BUT THE PREMISES OF FOOTBALL—IT'S A PHYSICAL GAME. IF YOU ENTERTAIN ANY CHANCE TO WIN, YOU MUST PLAY THE GAME PHYSICALLY—THAT HAS NOT CHANGED. IT WILL NEVER CHANGE.

John Robinson
USC Football

ABSOLUTE SILENCE. THAT'S THE ONE THING A SPORTSWRITER CAN QUOTE ACCURATELY.

Bobby Knight
University of Indiana Basketball

YOU CAN SAY SOMETHING TO POPES, KINGS AND PRESIDENTS, BUT YOU CAN'T TALK TO OFFICIALS. IN THE NEXT WAR, THEY OUGHT TO GIVE EVERYBODY A WHISTLE.

Abe Lemmons
University of Texas Basketball

I DON'T JOG. IF I DIE, I WANT TO BE SICK.

Abe Lemmons
University of Texas Basketball

151

I NEVER HAD A PHILOSOPHY OTHER THAN WHIP THE OTHER GUY.

Mike Ditka
Chicago Bears

I'M NOT MEAN AT ALL. I JUST TRY TO PROTECT MYSELF. YOU'LL SEE I DON'T EVER PICK ON ANYBODY WHO HAS A NUMBER ABOVE 30.

Mike Ditka
Chicago Bears

MAN, THIS IS WHAT FOOTBALL IS ALL ABOUT— PEOPLE GETTING THE SNOT KICKED OUT OF THEM!

Mike Ditka
Chicago Bears

FOOTBALL IS BLOOD, TEARS, SWEAT, PAIN.
IF YOU WANT SOMETHING ELSE, GO TO A
CHESS MATCH.

Mike Ditka
Chicago Bears

HE'S ONE MAN WHO DIDN'T LET SUCCESS GO
TO HIS CLOTHES.

Mike Ditka
Chicago Bears
Referring to former Oakland Raiders
coach-turned-broadcaster John Madden.

PLAYER WEIGHT IS THE MOST OVERRATED COMMODITY IN FOOTBALL. FRESHMEN CONSTANTLY COME IN HERE AND THINK BIGGER IS BETTER, BUT IT'S NOT. THEY CAN'T RUN, THEY CAN'T MOVE AND FATIGUE MAKES A COWARD OUT OF THEM.

Don Nehlen
West Virginia Football

COLLEGE FOOTBALL IS NOT A RELIGION. IT'S JUST A GAME. IT HAS A PLACE IN OUR SOCIETY, NO QUESTION, AND THE BENEFITS ARE GREAT IF IT'S APPROACHED IN THE RIGHT WAY. THE GAME IS REALLY AN INSTRUMENT THAT SHOULD BE USED IN A VERY POSITIVE, CONSTRUCTIVE WAY. STUDENT-PLAYERS WHO STAY THE COURSE WILL COME OUT OF HERE STRONGER, BETTER, MORE ETHICAL, BECAUSE WE PLAY BY THE RULES.

Joe Restic
Harvard University Football

THE MAN WHO COMPLAINS ABOUT THE WAY THE BALL BOUNCES IS LIKELY THE ONE WHO DROPPED IT.

Lou Holtz
Notre Dame Football

THE ONLY WAY I'D WORRY ABOUT THE WEATHER IS IF IT SNOWS ON OUR SIDE OF THE FIELD AND NOT THEIRS.

Tommy Lasorda
Los Angeles Dodgers

PUBLICITY IS LIKE POISON. IT DOESN'T HURT UNLESS YOU SWALLOW IT.

Joe Paterno
Pennsylvania State University Football

*THIS YEAR WE PLAN TO RUN
AND SHOOT. NEXT SEASON WE
HOPE TO RUN AND SCORE.*

Billy Tubbs
Texas Christian University Basketball

159

OPEN UP A BALLPLAYER'S HEAD AND YOU
KNOW WHAT YOU'D FIND? A LOT OF
LITTLE BROADS AND A JAZZ BAND.

Mayo Smith
Philadelphia Phillies

IF YOU MAKE EVERY GAME A LIFE-AND-DEATH PROPOSITION, YOU'RE GOING TO HAVE PROBLEMS. FOR ONE THING, YOU'LL BE DEAD ALOT.

Dean Smith
University of North Carolina Basketball

BALLPLAYERS ARE A SUPERSTITIOUS BREED, NOBODY MORE THAN I, AND WHILE YOU ARE WINNING YOU'D MURDER ANYBODY WHO TRIED TO CHANGE YOUR SWEATSHIRT, LET ALONE YOUR UNIFORM.

Leo Durocher
Chicago Cubs

GIVE ME SOME SCRATCHING, DIVING, HUNGRY BALLPLAYERS WHO COME TO KILL YOU.

Leo Durocher
Chicago Cubs

IF THEY THROW ONE AT YOUR HEAD, YOU THROW TWICE (AT THEIR HEADS). IF THEY THROW TWICE, YOU THROW FOUR TIMES.

Leo Durocher
Chicago Cubs
Advising his pitchers.

YOU DON'T SAVE A PITCHER FOR TOMORROW. TOMORROW IT MAY RAIN.

Leo Durocher
Chicago Cubs

MY PLAYERS CAN WEAR THEIR HAIR AS LONG AS THEY WANT AND DRESS ANYWAY THEY WANT. THAT IS IF THEY CAN PAY THEIR OWN TUITION, MEALS AND BOARD.

Eddie Robinson
Grambling University Football

THERE ARE THREE IMPORTANT THINGS IN LIFE: FAMILY, RELIGION AND THE GREEN BAY PACKERS.

Vince Lombardi
Green Bay Packers

THINGS GOT SO BAD THAT I HAD TO PLAY MY STUDENT-MANAGER FOR A WHILE. THEY GOT REALLY BAD WHEN SHE STARTED TO COMPLAIN TO THE PRESS THAT SHE WASN'T GETTING ENOUGH PLAYING TIME.

Linda Hill-McDonald
University of Minnesota Women's Basketball

STATISTICS ALWAYS REMIND ME OF THE FELLOW WHO DROWNED IN A RIVER WHOSE AVERAGE DEPTH WAS ONLY THREE FEET.

Woody Hayes
Ohio State Football

Other Titles by Great Quotations

301 Ways to Stay Young At Heart
African-American Wisdom
A Lifetime of Love
A Light Heart Lives Long
Angel-grams
As A Cat Thinketh
A Servant's Heart
Astrology for Cats
Astrology for Dogs
A Teacher is Better Than Two Books
A Touch of Friendship
Can We Talk
Celebrating Women
Chicken Soup
Chocoholic Reasonettes
Daddy & Me
Dare to Excel
Erasing My Sanity
Falling in Love
Fantastic Father, Dependable Dad
Golden Years, Golden Words
Graduation Is Just The Beginning
Grandma, I Love You
Happiness is Found Along The Way

High Anxieties
Hooked on Golf
I Didn't Do It
Ignorance is Bliss
I'm Not Over the Hill
Inspirations
Interior Design for Idiots
Let's Talk Decorating
Life's Lessons
Life's Simple Pleasures
Looking for Mr. Right
Midwest Wisdom
Mommy & Me
Mom's Homemade Jams
Mother, I Love You
Motivating Quotes for Motivated People
Mrs. Murphy's Laws
Mrs. Webster's Dictionary
My Daughter, My Special Friend
Only a Sister
Parenting 101
Pink Power
Read the Fine Print

Reflections
Romantic Rhapsody
Size Counts !
Social Disgraces
Sports Prose
Stress or Sanity
The ABC's of Parenting
The Be-Attitudes
The Birthday Astrologer
The Cornerstones of Success
The Rose Mystique
The Secret Language of Men
The Secret Language of Wome
The Secrets in Your Face
The Secrets in Your Name
TeenAge of Insanity
Thanks from the Heart
The Lemonade Handbook
The Mother Load
The Other Species
Wedding Wonders
Words From The Coach
Working Woman's World

Great Quotations Publishing Company
2800 Centre Circle
Downers Grove, IL 60515, U.S.A.
Phone: 630-268-9900   Fax: 630-268-9500